Oct 31, 2007

Wednesday: Coffee w. milk 2%
Cocoa Via breakfast bar
Apple
Cream of Potatoe Soup - Tabachnik
2 slices of Pizza
Milky Way, Mary Jane (2), Payday
Milk Duds
Spring Salad w. Vinaigrette Dress.
Roasted Chicken Slices, Avocado
Bacon Bits, Tomatoe

November 1, 2007

Coffee w. 2% Milk - 2 cups
Bagel w. Cream cheese & boysenberry
jelly.
Whole wheat & Spinach Spaghetti
w. 3 meatballs & gnocchi (3)
Chicken Cutlets (2) corn, mashed
potatoes Persimmon Bread
with tomatoe & olive oil.

Wednesday   Jan 2, 2008
Tea w. 1% Milk
Sugar Free Oatmeal (Instant)

Boiled Chicken Dumplings (8) w.
Soy Sauce

Hor'sDovre - Spinach Square (2)
              Potatoe Puffs (2)
              Mini Taco (1)
              Broccdi & Potato (3)

Spaghetti w. Meat Sauce
Chicken Soup w. Vegitables & Noodles
Bean Sprouts w. Italian Dressing

Thursday   Jan 3, 2008
Coffee w. 1% Milk - 2 ½ cups
Cream of Wheat w. Maple Syrup &
1% Milk

Tangerine
Chipotle Hummus w. Multigrain
Crackers
Chicken Soup w. Vegetables (2)

2 Small hamburgers (no bun)
Coffee w. 1% milk

Friday   Jan 4, 2008
Coffee w. whole milk
Special K cereal w. whole milk
Banana

Peppers, Onions & Tomatoes in
Olive Oil - Salad - Italian Bread
Sweet Potato - Baked

Pork Chop - Breaded
Coffee w. whole milk
Almonds
Hummus w. Multigrain crackers.

Saturday   Jan 5, 2008
Coffee w. milk (2%)

Pan Fried Meat Dumplings with
Soy Sauce + Sesame Oil

Maple Nut Candy + Peanut Brittle
Coffee w. whole milk
Chocolate Truffle

Roast Pork
Sausage Peppers + Onions + Potato
Challah Bread

Sunday   Jan 6, 2008
Coffee w. 2% Milk
Apple Danish

Rotisserie Chicken
1/2 whole wheat pita
4 Bean Salad
1 Pickle

Potato Chips

Monday   Jan 7, 2008
Tea w. milk 2%

Vegetarian Chilii — Tabachnik

Macaroni & Cheese — Tabachnick

Breaded & Fried Chicken Cutlet
Mashed Potatoes
Corn on The Cob

Guacomole Dip + Taco Chips &
Potato Chips
Coffee w- Milk

Tuesday   Jan 8, 2008
Coffee w. Milk
Biscotti

Tabachnik Chicken Soup w. Noodles
Sesame Crackers (6)
Werther's Sugar Free Candies (5)

Spinach Calzone (without cheese)
Tabouleh salad
Guacamole Dip + Chips (Tortilla +
Potato)

Roast Pork
Sausage, Peppers + Onion on
Italian Bread

Wednesday   Jan 9, 2008
Coffee w. 1% milk

Romaine Salad w. Ranch Dressing
Peppers + Bean Sprouts

Chicken Cutlet - breaded & fried
Mashed Potatoes
Roast Pork w. Sausage Peppers
+ Onions; Italian Bread

Mocha Coffee Nips - 3
Crackers (6) (sesame)
Biscotti - 4 (almond)

Thursday   Jan 10, 2008
Coffee w. 10% Milk

Sesame / Honey Candy (4)
Crackers (10)
Coffee w. whole milk

Salad w. Ranch Dressing +
Bacon Bits (Imitation)
Chicken Dumplings w. Soy +
Dumpling Sauce
Sauteed Cabbage w. Soy +
Olive Oil
Coffee w. whole milk

Potato Chips

Friday   Jan 11, 2008
Coffee w. 1% Milk
Organic Granola w. Pumpkin Seeds
Milk

Peanut Butter & SF Rasberry
Jelly on whole wheat (40 Cal)
per slice

Sesame Crackers

Hamberger on roll w. purple
onion, romaine littuce, ketchup
Potato Salad
Cashews & Dry / Salted Garbonzo

Sesame & Honey Candies
Coffee with Milk (1%)

Tangerine

Saturday   Jan 12, 2008
Coffee J w. 1% Milk
2 Scrambled eggs on pita bread

Stuffed Pepper w. Rice + Beef

Steak + Corn
Chicken Soup w. Vegetables
Fanch Fries
Banana

Cashews + Potato Chips
Green Tea

Monkey Bread + Coffee w. 1%

Sunday   Jan 13, 2008
Coffee w. 1% Milk
Cream of Wheat
1 Hard boiled egg

Roast Pork
Cabbage
Chicken Dumplings

Stuffed Pepper
Cashews & Potato Chips
Hummus & Tortilla Chips

Monday   Jan 14, 2008
Coffee w. 10/0 milk
Yucca cake

2 pieces of fried chicken
cabbage
potato chips

Sausage, peppers + onions
Roast Pork w. garlic
Bowl of chicken noodle soup

Tuesday   Jan. 15, 2008
Coffee w. 1% Milk

Yucca Cake

Cinnamon Coffee w. Reg. Milk

Frankfurters w. cheese (Mini)
Pita Bread
Potato Chips

2 Chocolate Peanut Butter Wafers
Chick Peas (dried & salted)
Ritz Crackers (about 25!)

Wednesday   Jan 16, 2008
Coffee w. 10% milk (2 cups)

Sesame / Honey candies (3)
Cinnamon Coffee / whole milk

Coffee w. milk (1%)

Dried chickpeas
1/2 Banana

Thursday   Jan 17, 2008
Tea w. milk
2 hard boiled eggs

Coffee w. milk

Mesculun Salad w. Tomatoes
+ Italian Fat Free Dressing +
Bacon Bits + bean sprouts.

Spinach Knish & Beets (Pickled)

Chicken Soup w. Vegetables,
Orzo, Cabbage, Carrots, Celery
Chicken Peppers

Sesame Crackers

Mini Cheese Hot Dogs

Friday   Jan 18, 2008

Saturday   Jan 19, 2008
Coffee w/ 1% Milk

Spinach Pizza
Guacamole Dip & Tortilla Chips
Mashed Potatoes

Spinach Knish
Broccoli Rabe w. garlic & Oil

Sunday   Jan 20, 2008
Coffee w 1% Milk

Baked Ziti w. Meatballs
Bread

French Toast & Fried Egg

Steamed Brocoli & Cabbage

Monday   Jan 21, 2008
Coffee w. 2% Milk

Coffee w. 2% Milk

Pretzels

Chicken Soup w. Vegetables
Bread & Meatballs in Tomato
Sauce

Potato Chips
Caramel Popcorn.

Tuesday   Jan 22, 2008

Tea w. whole milk

Lo Cal/Fat Cream of Chicken
Cup a Soup w. crackers

3 Biscotti Cookies